NIGERIA CULTURAL REVOLUTION

Freedom of the Politicians from Traditional Rulers and Religious Leaders

Chief Oluwole Adetula

Dr Emmanuel Oluwole Adetula

This book was printed in United States May, 2014

To order additional copies of this book:

Write to:

Emmanuel Tula Books

Mailing: P.O. BOX 1017 Lawndale, CA.90260

E-mail: tulatax@gmail.com

Website: www.christchannelnetwork.org

Nigerian Cultural Revolution

Emmanuel Oluwole Adetula is an Author of 26 other books, In this book, "Nigerian Cultural Revolution" The chapter begins from Page 8, from page 30 this book gives 14 Reasons why Divorce is the greatest issue affecting Nigerians in America, From page 48 Tula tells a Story about The Old Prophet and the Young Prophet, from page 53 he exposed the facts about Judaism, Christianity and Islam, and he ended the book on WHY AFRICAN CHURCHES SUFFERED GROWTH IN AMERICA from page 61.

Get your copy today direct at www.amazon.com

For questions about this book or to request a free copy:-

Write Dr. Emmanuel Oluwole Adetula

tulatax@gmail.com

P.O. BOX 1017 Lawndale, CA. 90260
USA

www.christchannelnetwork.org

CONTENTS

Searching for the truth is the most honorable ministry in this world and it's my most dangerous assignment, after you know the truth, it takes courage and a gift of a Writer or Orator to make it known to the public and money to get it to the people. The battle of Nigeria has shifted from the political fight between the Good luck people and the Bad luck people , the Nigerian battles has now becomes the battle of the gods, Say it Loud in the streets corners and the markets places to all the Sons and Daughters of the land areas that surround the two great rivers of Africa, let the Prince of the Niger and the Princess of Benue accepts the dawn of a new order of modernization and development of Nigeria, The trumpet of freedom and liberty has been sound, whosoever have an ear to hear let him hear . Let the freedom reign! Let the people go! **Emmanuel Oluwole Adetula**

ABOUT THE AUTHOR

Dr. Emmanuel Oluwole Adetula, Master of Arts in Divinity, Doctor of Philosophy in Social Work, Professional Trainings in Philanthropy, Conflict Analysis, Conflict Resolution, Mediation, Negotiation and Conflict Management from The Academy for Conflict and Peace building United States Institute of Peace Academy. Washington, DC. , La Sierra University School of Business, Riverside, California and Pepperdine University School of Law at the Straus Institute for Dispute Resolution. Malibu, California. Member Association of Business Executives, Member Association of Conflict Resolution, Member California Lawyers for the Arts.

Emmanuel Oluwole Adetula licensed in the state of California USA as a Realtor, CPA/IRS Tax Professional and Notary Public. Current Managing Partner at Emmanuel Tula Associates, Emmanuel Tula Tax Service and Here & There On Time Transports . Born in Owo , Ondo State of Nigeria . Prymary home at Ibadan, Oyo State Nigeria with Permanent Home at Los Angeles, California United States of America.   Website: www.emmanueltula.com

Emmanuel Adetula is the Founding President/CEO of Christ Channel Network, a bona-fide 501 c 3 nonprofit organization in United States since 2002, doing business as CCN House Community Development agency, providing housing to homeless individuals and families in USA and CCN Orphan and Vulnerable Children Center. Website: www.christchannelnetwork.org

He is also the President CCN CENTER FOR PEACE. Emmanuel Oluwole Adetula is an Author of 26 other books, available at online bookstores in paperback and in kindle editions around the world.

Nigerian Cultural Revolution

Modernization and development requires an orientation commensurate with the problems of the present, and not an attempt to resurrect ideas from societies of the distant past. Nigeria has come to a cross road and a junction of decision to make a radical sociopolitical change in the culture of our forefathers towards the elimination of religious and cultural institutions that control the federal republic of Nigeria.

The time has come to free Nigerian politicians from their masters; I mean the traditional rulers and the religious leaders, and let the Politicians come direct to the people to seek power in order to establish in Nigeria true democracy; "the government of the people by the people and for the people" If Nigeria borrows a system of government from the west and adopted major part of American system of governance, then Nigeria must be ready to follow the basic principles of democracy and let all Nigerians hold these truths **to be self-evident, that all men are created equal, that they are endowed by their Creator with certain unalienable Rights, that among these are Life, Liberty and the pursuit of Happiness with the separation of religion and tradition rulers institution from the governance principles of the state.**

To secure these rights in Nigeria, Governments that are instituted henceforth in Nigeria must derive their just powers from the consent of the governed, not from the Obis, the Obas the Emirs or from any form of religion. The current form of Government becomes destructive of these ends, it is therefore the Right of the People to alter or to abolish it, and those who make it difficult to do this by the consent of the people through their popular votes in elections to political leadership will have to deal with it through a revolution that will institute a new Government in Nigeria with total elimination of traditional rulers from Nigeria, it is the right of the people , it is their duty, to throw off a Government that derives its power from traditional rulers and religious leaders but not from the people of Nigeria in true democracy , in order to provide new Guards for the future security , stability and prosperity for the people — Such has been the patient sufferance of Colonies; and such is now the necessity which is constraining us now to alter the current system for the public good and for the generations to come.

The continued relevance of traditional authorities to the local government System in contemporary Nigeria remains a roadblock to progress and the time for its elimination is now. Prominent traditional rulers such as the Oba of Benin and the Alafin of Oyo have vehemently expressed their dissatisfaction with how traditional institutions and their rulers have been relegated to the background over the years , even the Sultan of Sokoto still have the mentality that he can rules Nigeria from his palace, but the people has to move past concerted efforts by traditional rulers to enhance their role in the local government and a great deal of insensitivity amongst modern elected local government councilors , Politicians must rise up to degrade the ego of tradition rulers ; the emirs , the Obis , the Obas , the Chiefs and their assigned advisory roles in relevant provisions should no longer be fully respected by politicians if Nigeria has to move forward in the 21st century.

The basic goal of government is to generate rapid increase in social wealth and its driving force is economic development not religion, there must be a separation between the governance of state and Nigeria religious institutions begin with demolition of churches and mosques from government houses, put a stop to Government sponsorship of Nigerians Citizens to holy pilgrimage of Jerusalem and Mecca, complete separation of Islam and Christianity from the governance of the state and elimination of Sharia laws , Cannon laws and Customary Courts from Nigeria constitution, the elimination of Sharia laws as both a political and ideological force in the country is now.

The Sharia laws and customary laws strength which is largely rooted in a widespread grassroots supports of the Emirs and the Imams for decades , monopolizing power and seeking to control the country's identity along their lines of ideology must be rooted out in the body politics of Nigeria.

Nigerian traditional ruler's cultures of ethnicity represent nothing rather than authoritarian oppression, technological backwardness and class exploitation, the time has come for Nigerian people to make a clean break with the past in order to address the most urgent demands of the present. Nigerian indigenous traditions and traditional institutions which for decades continue to enhance or impede the processes of scientific and political modernization because of the traditional authority systems and traditional rulers in Nigeria has failed to provide a universally accepted definition of a traditional system of authority because of the diversity in the political and administrative components of traditional systems in different parts of the country.

It is important to say that British rule was not forged on negotiations with Nigerians, but negotiations with ethnic nationalities represented by the traditional rulers, so also there was no "Nigerian people position," but ethnic nationality leadership positions. Nigeria nation started in 1960 with a

subtle blackmail that children should respect their parents because their opinion varies with the status quo.

For a century young Nigerians, well-brought up with cultural and religious values for respect of elders do have immense respect for elders but they cannot respectfully disagree and insist on their position , an attitude and cultural disposition which has continue to massage the egos of outdated cultures and traditions fit only to the waste basket of antiquity.

Colonialism violently disrupted African cultural traditions and imposed European forms of thought and social organization on the African colonized peoples. Having achieved political independence, postcolonial Africans must now pursue a more decisive social and economic liberation towards the decolonization of African minds and societies, genuine modernization in Africa can only be realized through the revitalization of African cultural norms and revitalization of its religious and cultural belief systems, The group of Nigeria that is qualified to carry out this cultural revolution are the youths of this country between the age of 18 and 40.

Nigeria cannot pretend to move forward into scientific, technological and economic development to compete in the global market and the new world order that is in the making by letting its time and resources be taken over by religious issues, the matter of religion should be left out of government budget and the time for the elimination of traditional rulers institutions is now.

The problem of Nigeria lies with the degree of decision prominence which the government gives to dynastic traditional rulers in the context of a gradually evolving local government system directed at popular representation, citizen participation and mobilization, and their role as informed observers and ceremonial participants in matters of local government is no longer needed, they deserve no more salaries but should get donations to support their ceremonial roles from their subjects.

The population of Nigeria has been projected to be 440.4 million by mid-2050 and 239.9 million by mid-2025. The country's population, as of the end of June 2013, is at 173.6 million. In 2050, Nigeria will be the third most populous country in the world, just behind India and China; this means that over the period of 37 years, Nigeria's population figures will overtake those of the United States of America, which will be 399.8 million in 2050.

In 37 years time a Nigerian youth between the age of 18 and 40 today will be between the ages of 55 and 87 years old , therefore if they don't fight now and change the social political order of the day put in place by their own fathers , they will suffer at my current age and they will not have the opportunity of becoming an immigrants in Europe or in America in 37 years time, and when they died , they will leave this country Nigeria in more bad shape politically, economically, socially , scientifically and technological bankrupt for their own children. We have been around this mountain for too long, it's time for the youth of this country to get a Joshua and cross the Jordan River to the other side of Nigeria new order for the sake of their own future and the generations to come.

The problem arising from the traditional rulers and religious leaders in the government system in Nigeria arose from the outdated traditions, custom and religious believers of the people which is in contradiction to modernity nexus in the present political, social and economic scheme of the modern world , these indigenous traditional institutions has become a road block to the challenges of contemporary democratic processes.

Nigeria traditional modes of thought, behavior and institutions constitute impediments to the projects of modernization and development in Nigeria. Nigeria is the only place that I know where someone thinks he is more superior than you all because he was born into this world before you, He wants to be respected and honor because of his age , but he has no commonsense to show for being an older person in the family. (Tell every Agbaiya that respects comes with responsibility not age). You work , he is busy praying from Churches to Mosques to Herbalist to get what his own brother works for through spiritual terrorism prayer methods, culturally and religious rogues senior brothers and Junior or Senior sisters, Wicked Aunts and Demonic Uncles who thinks you owe them something because you share the same family blood.

Nigeria traditional institutions and the religious leaders are anti-modernization, therefore promoting traditional rulers involvement in the political process has tied down Nigeria progress to the time of the advent of British rule in different parts of present day Nigeria , now the basic problem of Nigeria is the fact that the politicians still hold the believe that religious leaders and traditional rulers are still the repository of religious, legislative, executive and judicial functions of their lives which continue to make the traditional rulers and the religious leaders the nucleus of governance in Nigeria , though it may be argue that no traditional ruler or a religious leader have the geographical spheres of authority   or jurisdiction over the entire geographical area of modern Nigeria, but the truth is that all politics are local, a reason no politician can rise to the state or national level political office without the support of the local religious leader or the traditional ruler , therefore the politicians are voted into state and national positions through the influence of the local traditional rulers and the religious leaders , politicians don`t get to office by merit or the love to serve the people , it's all about who is the religious leader or a traditional ruler backing you up.

The institution of traditional ruler ship should be abolished, as it is an Anachronism in a democratically elected local government system, guaranteed under the Nigerian Constitution, Section 7(1) of the 1979, 1989 and 1999 Constitutions, and the parallel institution of traditional ruler ship is anomalous. if Nigeria as a country is serious about ensuring that the citizenry adopts the democratic and participatory culture needed to quicken the pace of modernization, then a decisive step needs to be taken to 'jettison this archaic institution once and for all' to enable the people develop the required orientation in line with the reality of the present age and time, the principles behind democratic local government and the institution of traditional ruler ship are opposed to each other; the solution advanced by them does not appear realistic.

For one thing, the high degree of acceptance of traditional authorities particularly in the rural areas cannot be dismissed as inconsequential, nevertheless traditional ruler ship easily obliterates rulers' legitimacy and public acceptance. Elimination of this institution can be confrontational and can create chaos in local government operations, but that is what

I call revolution, freedom of the politicians by the people from the traditional rulers and religious leaders, traditional ruler ship in Nigeria must be smashed, Let the splintered particles of the smashed system float in the macro and micro political processes. Their activisms have had adverse implications for the growth of genuine democracy as well as political modernization. Nigeria can no longer allow traditional functionaries and religious leaders to exercise corrosive influence clandestinely on Nigeria body politics, it is better to clothe them formally with illegitimacy disallowing their active involvement in party politics, they can only be relevant by serving as agents of transition from traditionalism to modernism by transforming their palaces to local public libraries .the traditional system is anachronistic, undemocratic, divisive and costly to Nigeria political process and as such a hindrance to the development and transformation of the continent of Africa.

In the North, the Emir could be referred to as a strong executive participator in local administration with no restraints on his executive powers. In the South West, beside the Oba (or king), there were other power blocks or centers such as the body of king makers, the town council and powerful secret societies whose input in shaping the local administration acted as checks on the Local government official, so the Oba can be regarded as executive participator in local administration.

In the South East, the indigenous political system reveals a great deal of popular participation , fragmented with authority from the household level to the village level .In all, the traditional ruler was an embodiment of local administration , the British colonial administrators recognized the strategic and influential position occupied by traditional rulers in the Nigeria and they used the system against the people of Nigeria to perpetuate into eternity to run the country in line with British colonial policy of running colonies and managing the volatile law and order , creating 1% masters and 99% slaves which still exist today , where the Obas, Obis and the Emirs with their political robots in office in collaboration with the western powers own 99% of the wealth while the 99% have to be fighting on the crumbs falling from their dining table.

The colonialists avoided attempting any drastic reforms of the indigenous local administration in Nigeria; instead, the British colonial administration took steps to put in place a system of indirect rule, as a convenient strategy to govern the people through their traditional rulers and religious leaders while ensuring close guidance by British Administrators. In this way, the allegiance of the people was secured via their traditional rulers and the religious leaders.

In effect, there was a clear attempt by the colonial government to consolidate the role of traditional rulers as chief executives of their localities, the traditional rulers were in firm control of their local councils and they tended to be despotic and authoritarian in performing their functions which were essentially maintenance of law and order, and enforcement of tax policies of the British colonial government. By mid 1940s however, political parties in the country had begun to assert themselves.

Nationalists were forceful in demanding adequate representation in government affairs, while at the same time pressing for self-rule. They contended that the existing

Native Authority System was incompatible with modern secular and democratic tenets of local government. About this time too, the British government was reappraising its strategy of governance at the local level with the aim of evolving a system of democratic and efficient local government.

Nigeria has around 173m people, of whom about 44 per cent are under the age of 14, this under 14 years old 44 per cent in 30 years time when 60 per cent of current leadership are old and deal will be under the age of 44, and Nigeria traditional rulers institution is based on mobs of syndicated killers or head hunters called RITUALIST with Stories of human body parts factories in the hands of these ritual killers making this nation to continue to be plagued by epidemic of corruption and a catalogue of horrors where body parts of the Nigerian victims were being removed, they were carefully packaged and kept for some individuals who comes to this villages with exotic cars to receive the consignment of human body parts, mind you not body parts from mortuaries body from the use of human body parts which traditional sacrifice of our fathers still believes for sacrifice which can increase the chance of becoming extremely wealthy.

The customs and tradition of which this traditional institution is based is used to acquire some spiritual powers against enemies and also would help to project one into business and political hierarchy. As Nigerians are caught on the web of material madness and political aggrandizement, so they continue to kill people secretly for human sacrifice, all these is happening before the very eyes of traditional rulers who cannot be separated from the ritualism, and they sell these Nigerian body parts to western doctors who come from United States who would receive Nigeria body parts to treat their own citizens and give them better life.

17

Nigerian Cultural Revolution

Young Nigerian ladies were simply captured to produce babies that would eventually be used for money rituals or for medical body parts to better the lives of Western worlds Citizen in their advance medical clinics, the price of a cow is not less than 100,000 naira in Nigeria, but Nigerians have been reduced to mere walking elements without any significant value. They are robbed and dehumanized by politicians, hunted by religious extremists, robbed, killed and sold as body parts at free will by ritualism operating under the outdated cultures and traditions and customs which these traditional rulers represented in Nigeria. There was a man named; Gazali admitted that he had been in the business of selling human parts for years. He went further to say that it was always easier for him to sell live human beings which cost 40,000 naira than the human parts.

The confessions of Gazali simply validate the fact the life of a Nigerian is now less than the value of a cow. And 40,000 is about $250. What Nigeria traditions, customs and the belief of our forefathers stood for in today's world is that the life of a Nigerian is worth $250, these rituality are divided into various groups. The man who wants to become powerful or rich, the voodoo man who is ready to prescribe the human sacrifice and the kidnapper who is prepared to provide the scapegoat. The victims are magically hypnotized and rendered into a defenseless state of zombies before their final moment on earth. And if you escape, where will you go, to the church where the false prophets and false teachers also are agents of the ritualism, and if you even hide in Mosque, the Alfas are worse Ritualist in Nigeria, these people of worse than BOKO HARAM, these ritualism, prophets and Alfas have become weapons of mass destruction spreading their tentacles across the country.

When people are devoid of any sense of moral justice, and have chosen to make evil the sentinel of their lives, then this situation in Nigeria has now reached a climax and the time to put a stop into everybody reaping the dividend of evil, wickedness, atrocities, maliciousness, selfishness and ungodliness of the very few is now, we can no longer afford to continue to be in a world of perpetual fear and uncertainty because we want to protect an outdated culture and tradition of our forefathers, every masquerades must go into the museum of history and never rear its head on street of liberty and freedom of this new nation.

We can no longer continue to be a nation of small minds governed by small minds. We have to move into modernization of commonsense, compassion and humanity, where the poor have hope, freedom and liberty and the pursuit of happiness and no longer eat from the dustbins and wear second hand clothes. A nation where truth is not mocked ridiculed and treated with contempt and where falsehood, hate, deceit and misrepresentation are no longer exalted. A nation where eighty year old men is no longer described as promising and dynamic leaders and wise men taking seven year old girls as wives as Obis, Obas and Emirs, This is evil. This generation must end it, and put traditional rulership in the museum of history and turned the Emirs, the Obas and the Obis Palaces into public library and local museums from East to West and North to the South. This is what I called People`s government of the people for the people and by the people.

From whence does the enemy derive the strength that enables him to remain entrenched in human society? Why is it so difficult to eradicate these pockets of evil in our social structures? Why do they defy the attempts made by sincere and earnest men and women, such as are recorded in our daily newspapers week after week, to eliminate or control these problems? Why are they so hard? Why is it that the application of good, sound, commonsense principles does not seem to solve the situation? Why is it that the parties involved cannot sit down and talk out their differences amicably and helpfully? Why does it all seem to suddenly explode in riot and demonstration and violence? Why are race problems so explosive? Here is another area where violence seems to tremble beneath the surface of almost every meeting that is called to try to discuss these problems. Why is this? We must ask these deep questions if we are going to understand the enemy we attack.

One of the chief rules of warfare is, know your enemy. You can never be successful as a soldier if you do not know something of the tactics of the enemy. This is true in military conflict and it is true in spiritual warfare as well. The second rule of warfare is, know your weapons. Know what you have to meet the enemy with, and know how to use them. Nigeria enemy is not IBO vs. HAUSA vs. YORUBA to keep Nigeria one is a task that must be done. The most effective way to influence behavior is to influence thinking. Satan did that to Adam and Eve in the garden of Eden - doubting God's truth; The truth is that Ibadan people does not see themselves as same as the Ijebus, that was confirmed during the 1983 after elections riot when Akinjide and Akinloye were shooting people at sight in Ibadan claiming all Ijebus should leave Ibadan, has Ibadan's changed, what is Owo people attitude now as to their daughters marrying Ondo girl?

To solve Nigeria problem, there must be an elimination of all traditional rulers and the religious leaders to pave way for a new modernization of a society that will embraces science and technology above the traditions and customs of our traditional rulers that is fit only in dustbin basket of antiquity and let us convert the palaces of the emirs, the obis and the obas to local museums and public libraries.

When a movement begins as an emotional outburst it is rather simple to control. At that early stage of any movement it can be easily handled. Those involved can usually sit down with others and work out things, and, as emotions cool, wiser heads prevail. This happens all the time. There are incipient movements around us that are being arrested at their very start by such processes. But when a movement passes to the second stage and begins to be supported and buttressed by arguments, by reasoned defenses and explanations in justification of these things, from that moment it begins to take on strength and is difficult to overthrow.

This is exactly what happens today. A movement begins -- certain conditions create it -- and there is an emotional reaction to it. Then, instead of calming down so that the problems can be worked out, somebody defends that action. Someone writes out an argument for it, or speaks about it, and justifies it. Soon the movement spreads and it is then very difficult to overthrow. It has derived strength from "reasoning's."

But now we must look at this more closely, we must understand what these reasoning's are, for they are, essentially, a tribute to the primacy of the mind, the intelligence, in man. What distinguishes man from the animals is that he refuses to have his mind bypassed.

21

Animals react emotionally; they follow urges, the instincts of their own kind. When an animal acts he is not troubled by conscience. He does not toss and turn all night in his sleep because of what he did during the day -- you can check them and see.

Men would react the same way if it were not for the mind, that strange faculty of wanting everything to be logical, reasonable, and justifiable. Thus it is the mind that prompts the conscience. The mind cannot be bypassed; it must come into play. But when it is asked to defend something that is not right (i.e., is not in line with reality), then these reasoning's become false reasoning's. They become what we call rationalizations. They are simply an expedient that the mind resorts to, to make an action that has already occurred appear to be reasonable.

This is where evil derives its strength. It produces specious and plausible sounding arguments which make their ultimate appeal to man's self-sufficiency, his unlimited capabilities (as he sees himself), These things appeal to man's independence, so logically and compellingly, that millions are deceived by them and follow them. That is why evil is so deeply entrenched in society.

Let us go a step further: In the full revelation whence these reasoning have come, the ultimate source of them. Without going into this in any detail I want to pinpoint them for you. "Doctrines of demons." He says they arise from "seducing spirits," spirits at work, using the minds of men as their instruments, to present to humanity what are really lies. They are reasonable-sounding lies, plausible lies, but they are actually lies, they are not truths. They are false, seductive, they lead people astray. They do not educate the mind toward truth but toward error.

Nigerians cannot govern themselves under the current leadership,

Terrorism always gains sanctuary in ungoverned spaces and start to build a terrorist infrastructure, and then the threat of the terrorist launching attacks grows. With Boko Haram kidnapping of some 270 school girls and threats to sell them into sexual slavery is a clear indication that the battles of Nigeria has shifted from a fight between the good luck people and the bad luck people and it has now becomes a battle of the gods, a truth which has now sparked international outrage, leading to pledges of assistance to Nigeria. France has once again offered its help, China is willing to share satellite imagery that might help locate the militants, and Britain has offered its Special Air Service commandos and surveillance aircraft. USA is sending a multiagency counterterrorism team that includes FBI hostage negotiators and investigators, intelligence analysts, and up to 10 uniformed personnel from the U.S. Africa Command to assess the military needs of the Nigerian security forces. The mass kidnapping of children, combined with other recent attacks — including a bombing in a bus station in Nigeria's capital of Abuja that killed more than 70 people and a massacre at an open-air market in the northern city of Gamboru Ngala that reportedly killed more than 300 civilians has crossed a new threshold of lethality and depravity that there is a political power vacuum in this ungoverned nation of Nigeria , the power that govern Nigeria is hidden behind religion and traditional rulers institutions , not the political power led by the President of the Country. The only supplies Nigeria security forces have in abundance at the army barracks are ingredients for the officer mess pepper soups. A Nigerian soldier or Police man or a member of Nigerian Security forces who died as a result of trying to save another Nigerian will be a laughing stock to the rest Nigerians because Nigeria is a country that has no place for Heroes , the only person Nigerians respect and honor is a person with money, big mansions , expensive cars and high costs clothes and attires, Nigerian culture put the Nigerian military and the security forces in a corner not to want to die in an efforts to save another Nigerians, there is no place for heroic achievements in Nigerian, even at the family level, you are not respected by your own family members if you don`t have the money, and when you brought the money home , nobody care how you got it?, everybody want money and they do not care how they got it and who is killed in the process because Nigerian society will never question you on how you got your wealth, so what everybody are chasing is how do I get money today, Nigerians don`t care whosoever is hurt in the process of getting the money today!, so the Police , The Military and The Security forces becomes parts of the culture of Bribery , corruption,   stealing, dishonesty, killing your own brothers and sisters for money , nobody will questions you, nobody is going to ask you how you got it, how did you make it, they will all honor you, love you because you have the money, respect you, welcome you, just give them the money, they will celebrate you, money, money, money is the root of all the trouble in Nigeria, it's not only Boko Haram that sells girls for $12 per person, Nigerian will sell even their own child for $12 . Nigeria is the only place that I know where a mother want her child dead in a foreign land in order for her to take over her Son property in Nigeria , it is a country where the whole community will support you for getting what belongs to another person , a country where Church Pastors and Mosques Alfas will be praying for you so that your husband will die in order for you to take over your spouse properties, they will vote for you as long as you got the money, it doesn't matter if you steal or kill someone in their presence on order to get the money, just share them out of the money, Nigerians calls it prayer answered not wickedness, when you operate in a society like that , there is no way you can deny the militants local support if they are giving you little money to hide in your own house particularly in a nation that the security forces lack rudimentary capabilities such as adequate ammunition for their guns, and they can accept open bribe at the airport to sneak terrorist in and out of the country.

When you look for the demonic, do not merely look at the occult, at the realm of outright demonic possession, etc. These "wicked spirits in high places" we wrestle against these who are working through the minds and thinking of men. How else can you explain the evil that keeps cropping up in human society? Why is it that universities, dedicated to the pursuit of truth, should become in many cases the places where evil is most deep-seated and most powerfully disseminated? How else can you account for this, except that correctly analyzed the situation and that these ideas come from demonic spirits working through the minds of men, teaching wrong ideas in a very logical and plausible manner.

Try that formula out on life and see if it does not fit. Every movement has its reasoning's to support it -- the good as well as the bad, the true as well as the false. Each has its philosophy, its defenders, its explainers, its theologians, if you like, who are constantly justifying and explaining why things happen. But you can tell the difference between the good and the bad, between truth and error, when you see what is at the heart of it, what is the thrust of it, what is behind it which men are trying to bring out.

Then, look at the heart of any philosophy, at its arguments and reasoning's: but does it exalt man? That is the point. If it is lifting up man as something high and great, something that exalts itself, praises itself that is the test. When you see what lies behind these things, then you can tell whether it is a doctrine of demons or the truth

What lies behind race prejudice, whether it is white or black? It is becoming very apparent that there are as many black racists as there are white, proportionately. What lies behind that? You can see clearly it is a desire for pride, for domination over others, for the exaltation of "my group" as opposed to someone else's group. Racism is always this, and, therefore, it is clearly a doctrine of demons. These reasoning have, no matter how plausible the arguments may sound in support of them, are revealed at their heart as being "high things" exalting themselves against the knowledge of God.

What is behind student unrest, violence, and riots, in our day? There is a degree of legitimate protest, granted. But when it moves in the realm of violence, when it becomes a mob, smashing and burning and looting and defying authority, it reveals itself to be motivated by a love of power, pride of will, loving to pit will against will, glorying in defiance of authority.

We are to bring the weapons of truth, love, righteousness, and faith to bear, because they destroy reasoning's. They pull down arguments; they demolish them, and the pride behind them. How does it all happen? I am not talking now merely of preaching, or teaching the truth, or handing someone a Bible, or a Koran. Remember the city of Corinth, where the people were buttressing their lives of immorality, shame, sordidness, and pagan barrenness, by arguments, and reasoning's. Tula is telling you now "When I come to you, I will not come to debate with you. I will not come with the wisdom of this world. I will not come to cancel out your arguments with a counter-argument. I will not come to debate philosophy.

I came to declare to you that there is a relief, release, and deliverance from the pride of the human heart , it s time for you to find a compassion awakening in your heart that has never been there before for your neighbors, your friends, and others who struggle on in the painful problems of life. You have the solution in your hands, I will come to set the people free from themselves, from their selfishness, and began the healing of life, the flowing of rivers of water, the refreshment of joy, and the fulfilling of life, the time is against me now, I cannot follow you to make another round trip around this mountain after 40 years round about journey, let's move forward and cross over the Jordan river, if the elders don`t want to go, let them die in this wilderness, the elders were baptized in the Red Sea and it's time for their children to get their own baptism in the Jordan river, the time is now!.

In Nigeria today I am considering how I should react to the social ills and injustices of our day. I suppose there has never been a time when these disorders of society were more widespread. They press upon us every way we turn and we cannot escape them. We need therefore to find an answer to these problems, two things are immediately evident: One is that we cannot and we must not ignore these problems. We must not try to evade them or ignore them. We must not try to run away from life. It is basically unmanly to run away from the problems of life, to seek a shelter where we can live out our years in Diaspora without encountering the difficulties around us. This was not the case with Jesus Christ and the Prophets. They lived square in the middle of life. They lived life up to the hilt and associated with those afflicted with grievous problems, emotionally, physically, and in every other way. This is also where every real man must live. We live in the world. We must not adopt a head-in-the-sand attitude. These bodily ills concern us, or they ought to. Second, it is apparent that we do not and must not attack these social problems in the way the world does. "We live in the world but the weapons of our warfare are not worldly." We do not face life the same way. We fight in another dimension, and yet our fighting is not weak; it is powerful. It wins, it succeeds, and it is mighty. We are faced with places and situations where evil is entrenched, where it cannot be dislodged easily, it is powerfully defended. They abound around us on every side. Many have become issues which the world is struggling vainly to alleviate, but without success. My way to fight will be to destroy arguments and every proud obstacle to the knowledge of God`s good plan for this land and give deliverance to majority of our people, and take every thought captive to obey the change that God want for the people of Nigeria, in which all Nigerians will find a fulfillment of their hopes and aspirations and unshaken guarantee of peace, freedom, liberty, stability and prosperity. I wrote this book in heaven, Published it in America to be distributed in Nigeria, I was able to do this because I am a Nigerian Citizen by Birth, American Citizen by Naturalization and a Citizen of the Kingdom of God by adoption , I have a Key to my own home in Nigeria , a Key to my own home in United States, and God has given me the keys to the kingdom of heaven, whatever I bind here on earth will be bound in heaven, and whatever I lose here on earth will be loosed in heaven. Whosoever is born by a Nigerian is a Nigerian, whosoever is born by an American immigrant system is an American and whosoever is born of God is god, therefore I am a Nigerian, I am an American and I am a god. Only about 10% of us in this world possessed the privilege of this kind, and to whom much is given, much is expected, therefore whatever

God has assigned me to do or say or write, I will be failing in my calling for fear of the 17,500 Nigeria public officers who pockets more than 75 per cent of a country's earnings, and gives the rest 175 million of the people only 25% under fundamentally defective constitutional arrangement. I will not quit because of the reports of the 500 wise men and women of the national conference , I will not shut my mount or stop the flow of ink from the fountain of my pen because of people opposition, persecution, hatred or because of my own weakness by the popular political police. I am weak but not wicked, God chose me, God called me, God appointed me and God anointed me for a time like this, 90% of the time, you are not going to be receive by those you are sent to help, but I will do what God has appointed and destined me to do before I go back home in peace.

The greatest Sin God will not forgive a nation is that God sent a man to you but you rejected him, If God want to help a nation He sent them a man. The battle of Nigeria has shifted from the political fight between the Good luck people and the Bad luck people , the Nigerian battles has now becomes the battle of the gods, Say it Loud in the streets corners and the markets places to all the Sons and Daughters of the land areas that surround the two great rivers of Africa, let the Prince of the Niger and the Princess of Benue accepts the dawn of a new order of modernization and development of Nigeria, The trumpet of freedom and liberty has been sound, whosoever have an hear to hear let him hear . Let the freedom reign! Let my people go!

14 Reasons why Divorce is the greatest issue affecting Nigerians in America

Divorce is now the greatest issue affecting Nigerians in America 60% of the marriages now is breaking down leading towards a bitter separation between the spouses , most of these marriages is under a tragic dimension of spouses killing their spouses themselves or the women going from churches to churches praying to God asking God to help them kill their spouses since it is only God in America who can commit homicide or murder and go free, because God has no home address in America, if you think is this church, after you stay there for some time and never see him except the Pastor who want to fuck you because you told him your husband is a bad man, then you go searching him in another church, only to found out that God is not an American, and hope that God lives in Nigeria, they sent money to Nigerian prayer contractors to help them kill their own spouse, thanks to Pastors, and Prophets from Ghana and Nigeria who comes to America weekly for revival to harvest dollars from Nigerian women giving them false hope of deliverance from normal disagreements between spouses that were allowed to develop into quarrels, estrangements, divorce and then fatal vengeance leading to deaths or grievous bodily harms which always boils down most of the time to the root of all evils…money. This cuts across all ethnic groups in Nigeria and even many African nationalities living in America. According 6 in every 10 marriages between Nigerian couples end in divorce in America for the following reasons.

1. Many of Nigerian men, especially those that have been in this country for a while, say 14- 20 years and having passed through the eye of a needle to get situated in this

country finally want to settle down with a 'home girl'. Some of the men went through African American women problems already to get his green card and citizenships through marriages just like Jacob married Lea ... Laban daughter in a foreign land to get his green card , despite the fact that he did not like her, So after years in a foreign land , Abraham still decided to go back and find a wife for Isaac from his home country despite the fact that there is already a lots of disconnections about what marriage to African women is all about after you have been in America for many years, after you have become "a new set of Africans with white man eyes".

You have forgotten that Nigerian women are quite different from western women. Nevertheless they marry into frictions between two cultures under the same roof, and Nigerians can understand American system unless She went through the system by herself, and the greatest spiritual insult you subject yourself to in America is to go to a church and allow yourself to be taught by a visiting Preacher from a village who have no clue on how this system works. God left America long time ago with Washington and Adam, you can come from the village to tell us here how this system works. You want to stay with your husband here in America; the best class to go is not the village preacher's class from Ghana or Nigeria. Now tell me after your 5 years prayers, night vigil, from church to church, crusades to seminars etc, the man still left you and your prophets and prayer contractors has not been able to kill him , and he is still here by himself and the white man you thought will be your better husband then , only want to test drive a black ass but will never own one, now loot at the mirror, too much prayer and fasting is aging you now and these men in the church do not want you but your own daughters?.

2. Another cause of the problem is that some men after staying in western countries for many years pursuing their careers, when they are ready to get married they go home to Nigeria. Most of them are in their late forties or late fifties. Some men, when they were leaving Nigeria for foreign countries, they believed that they would find everlasting love abroad and would not like to have anything to do with the girlfriends they left behind. But after searching for years, these brothers found out that America do not have angels as spouses, then they finally come home to get married, the ladies of their age brackets are no longer available or too old for them. , since they come for short vacation, they get married by recommendation. Some of their family members would line women up for him to pick from many variables like One time with King , you choose your own Esther whose purpose is to use you to advance her own parental Medical agenda for recommending the lady which is different from getting an husband but saving the Jews from his homegrown terrorist. Moreover, the better qualities then for marriage are mostly in their twenties, who are young enough to be their daughters. A generational gap between these spouses that creates lots of tensions, old enough to be their grand fathers. Time has changed! Women are now so liberated that a 20 year old in this 21st century is not the same as a 20 year old in the 20th century. Present women in their 20s are mostly exposed to lots of western cultures no thanks to the internet, pop cultures, movies, cable news etc. They now want more and demand in marriage. They demand more than what their grandmothers demanded during their time. These cause lots of frictions in marriages

when the new found sweet 16s come to live with the husband America. The issue of being about to satisfy her sexually is not the problem now, thanks for Viagra, cialis etc, it's never going to be about sex or child bearing, the main problem here is that there are lots of value differences

3. The values differences now involve what the man in his generation likes and what the young lady in her computer/internet generation likes. There is this incompatibility. The man may like classical music, while the girl likes rap, the man may like African delicacies which the girl likes to explore western delicacies and so on. Many succeed in marrying women much younger than they are, the lady may appear to be a Christian, but trust me, when she comes in as wives, she will cut off TBN and all these Christians TV channels, she need HBO all the time, trust me, she is not spiritual at all at 20s, 30s, you are old school, somebody need to grow young again or somebody is about to die in this house.

4. Some of these men in America has nothing in Nigeria and they have nothing also in United states but when they travel home, they paint a cozy picture of life in the America ;the kind of life that every lady back in Nigeria can only dream about. They pamper these prospective wives and buy them everything they want. They make them to believe that living in America is next to paradise! Most of these ladies are the cream of the crop back home. Under normal circumstances, they will never date these men if they are not living rich and living in America, who wants to be with

a Daddy with no Sugar. They can only persevere because they have found rich men (as they thought) as husbands. These ladies feel betrayed when they arrive America and see for themselves that the streets of America are not plated with dollars. How can you marry old men twice your age as classy , pretty, intelligent, smart and have very good jobs back in Nigeria because you got lied to by these men and got so much enticed with the prospect of marrying these men that you were ready to lose everything you have or worked for in Nigeria , and he got you pregnant before you come over here for fear that you would decamp once you come to learn that the ideal man is a fake after all, that she is just a security guard on $8 an hour with his PhD, saved this homecoming dollars for 10 years before he come get you, and he never told you he previously married to one crazy African American woman with kids to get a green card and he is already paying child support from his $8 an hour job with direct deductions by the department of social justice When they new wives come from Nigeria, they find out the truth. It now becomes a problem since the wife would not want part of her money to pay for a child support of the other woman she does not even know or heard about, then all the wine carrying and church wedding in Nigeria becomes betrayal after the cross-over to USA only find out that most things that she assumed about her man or about America appear not to be the case. The man is too old for me, he is married to another woman before, he had children by another woman, she is broke, poor, disgusted, she is black, she has an accent, she told me lies, at least if she has told me the truth, I will know what I am getting into, but Sister nobody told you the truth, now you see the truth yourself, that how it works in America, nobody tell you the truth about America, you have to know it for yourself.

5. This man lives in a dilapidated one room apartment in South Central Los Angeles or in Compton or in the most ghetto area in America, but at least there is 24 x 7 electricity and water supply and food are available cheap in the nearby superior market, at least you don`t get that in Nigeria, you better sit down and work the system and don`t start wasting your time going from churches to churches because God moved out from here long time ago. Deal with it and stop this accusations and counter accusations, and to let you know, there is nothing your mother is going to do to help you out of this, just go and bring her from Nigeria to help you take care of your babies, at Another problem is that many Nigerian men that want to get married to Nigerian ladies put the issue of money before love. We have these situations of Nigerian men targeting Nigerian ladies that are in the nursing schools, pharmacy schools and medical school. They care less about whether there is love or not between them. They go after nurses, pharmacists and doctors. They get married for wrong reasons, which is for the wife to come over here, pass her board exam and make quick money for him.

6. Some Nigerian men treat their wives that they 'imported' from Nigeria like their slaves or their personal business empires. Some, after helping their new spouses through Nursing Schools, they now see them as their meal tickets. There was a story that had it that a certain Nigerian man used to collect her wife's pay checks at the entrance to their

house. The story had it that whenever the wife got paid, the man would wait for her at the door and forcefully take the pay check she received. Some men grow very lazy immediately the wives complete their training in nursing and start working. The men would stop working as hard as he used to do or even work at all. They now prefer to work part time and depend almost solely on the wives income. Some will be traveling to Nigeria at every little notice to 'enjoy' the fruit of their labor. They see them as their entitlements or investments. My background in the law and law enforcement exposed me to a lot of Nigerian men that get locked up in US jails over domestic violence and other related cases. Many Nigerian men I see in jail over the period of my research were locked up over silly monetary issues, some were very ridiculous. The common complain I hear almost every time from these men that got involved in domestic violence and get locked up in jail is always: "After all I did for her, after putting her through nursing school, she is now making more money and she wants do dominate me. This is how she is going to pay me back after I brought her to this country, I took care of her and her family"

7. Nigerian single men work hard every day in America. They are used to working two jobs, they put their wives through schools; However, some men become lazy after their wives start working and making money. Most Nigerian women, especially those of them in the medical fields, work very hard. Some of them put 16hrs of work every other day to maximize their ability to bring fat checks home. But some men see them as their money makers. They left everything for these hard working women to take care of. These

women start to pay mortgages and all the bills that the men used to pay. Some men take off to summer vacation in Nigeria every year to catch some fun back home in Nigeria. Many of them quit their jobs and depend on their wives' incomes to pay for the house, the bills and taking care of the men responsibilities at home, the women now come to a decision by asking herself, ' what did I have an husband for in the first instance? Just for Sex?, I could have go out and have the Sex with any man I like out there, and one day She get caught, and that sets up the domestic warfare, and you cannot really accused her because you did not really caught her in the act. The Nigerian women in America have their own share of the problem.

There is this fallacy that this problem is prevalent among female Nigerian nurses. However, the main issue is that many women from Nigeria become nurses when they come to USA irrespective of whatever their professions were back home in Nigeria. Many women while they were single and living in Nigeria fall victim to material wealth. Many of them look at the men's pocket when they come to 'toast' them or ask for their hands in marriage. The mere fact that a guy is based in USA is enough requirements for getting her. Irrespective of what kind of person the man is or what kind of job he does for a living in America is immaterial to her. There are no more questions! Everything is based on assumption. Even relatives do not care anymore to ask questions because immediately a man touts his 'credential' as living abroad, many relatives see dollar signs everywhere. Her mother would want to go to America for on the excuse of helping her daughter to take care of grand baby infants. The father will dream of getting a car and getting help in training the other siblings of his daughter. No one will ask any question about the prospective son-in-law. It is as a result of the economic condition back home that cheapens our value system. Every lady's dream is to marry a rich man, after all their parents went through to train them, they do not want to continue to struggle. So when they finally settle with the supposedly rich guy living in America, they become disappointed when they come over here to live in America, Some do not care how old their prospective husbands are or whether she has any atom of love for their husbands provided the dollars are there. Some even harbor the ambition of ending the marriage immediately they come to the states and receive their green cards.

Her plans was to marry the guy, come over to the states, get her green cards and then leave the man to marry her boyfriend she left in Nigeria that was back home in Nigeria and bring him over to America. Some women back home in Nigeria have hardly seen a dollar back in Nigeria, but when they comes here, and after the husband put her through school and she starts making money; she will want the husband to turn into her house boys. When some of them get their salaries for the first time, they start to make naira conversion of the dollars! They start seeing themselves as millionaires in Nigeria. When they start sharing financial responsibilities with their husbands, they start seeing themselves as breadwinners and now the boss. There will no longer be respect to their husbands just because they see money.

8. Many Nigerian men want to avoid the expenses of going to Nigeria and the process of immigration getting a wife to America, they decide to marry Nigerian women here in America with no love, since the Nigerian women here want to marry you too as long as you are single, because their religious mentality is that they only want sex within the contest of marriage, so if you want a Nigerian women

in America, all what you need to do is just go to her prayer meeting church where she goes to pray for husband twice a week, and propose to her , get a $35 ring and tell her Ghana prophet and pastor that you want to marry her, then she open up everything for you , since all of them has become Lady Evangelist having been living between jobs and church for long time, love or no love you can get it cheap, you don't have based your judgment on whether there would be a lasting marital relationship , just based it on business judgments.

Marriage is business and saved sex or holy matrimony in Nigerian men marrying Nigerian women in America. You know you are doing it because you have both got disoriented about stories about wives 'imported' from Nigeria that come here and kick the man out after getting what she want. Many men do not want to fall victim of that , so they go for already established women in America , she already got everything, a house, 2 cars in the garage, making $10,000 a month on a 16th hour overtime job, in between church and workplace, all she need is holy sex from a man she can call her own man, she ask nothing except a ring and her pastor/prophet approval, she already outgrown her own parental approval anyway, you just need to come in and share in her wealth, lucky you, you may have to move in with her . You are very lucky if she is Nurse, pharmacist or in nursing school and she can cook, and you are still single, then somebody who want to die just meet somebody who is looking for somebody to kill, then the marriage is sealed only to end so soon because it was based entirely on business consideration, the woman want it because she want save sex or holy sex but the man wanted it because it is financially secured for him. Also there is a pride of place or competition between which wife was 'imported' from Nigeria and which wife was already here prior to marriage.

Some women that got married after they have already been in the states see themselves as gold. Some feel so important and self-assured that there is nothing the man can do to her since she was already a self made lady. Some think that they know too much and that they are better than 'imported' ones. There was a lady boasting that: "I'll kick him out of the house if he acts stupid, after all he didn't parcel me here from Nigeria". Some think that since they came here on their own and been to the states before her man married her, that she knows too much about US laws protecting women. They challenge their men to do their worse. When the husband packs out of the house, the lady may not be able to pay for the mortgage alone or carter for the kids no matter how much they won against the man for child support.

9. Another problem is that of third party influence. Most marital tragedies are caused by relatives on both sides. Some women let their mom that came to look after their kids for them while she works to run their marriage. The couple may be living happily until the wife's mother comes from Nigeria. When these parents come to USA and find out how much money her daughter makes every month, they will start thinking that their daughters are now the head of her husbands' family. Many marriages break up due to parent-in-law problems friends, false teachers, false prophets and village pastors doctrines influence. Most people get off well in their marriages as they come to understand each other. They have fashioned out a system that works for them taking into consideration the kind of society we find ourselves in. However, when one of their

parents or relatives visit them, thing start to change. Some men start to behave differently for fear of being seen as weak and a liar, the wife already adjusted to the reality of the lies told him by her husband in order to get her into the marrying him, now here come the husband family visitors who is complaining that the man is treating his wife as if she is her boss, Hey Fool; this is America! Get out of my house, he is my equal here, but for other men, in order to show that they are in charge, they start to command or boss their wives around.

They demand them to do certain things that were not the case before their august visitors came. They give their parents some reasons to step in and hijack their domestic affairs. Then my husband has changed , first complain to friends , then to church people, then to visiting herbalist bishop from the village here for 7 days revival, Many fall victims to some disgruntled people whose marriage were broken and who hate to see other people succeed in their own marriage. Many men start to listen to external advice whenever they have a little domestic issue with the wife. They forgot that no two marriages are the same. That one marriage fails does not mean that the other would fail also. Some men try to intimidate their wives immediately they come from Nigeria in order to 'cut her tails' because of the fear that she might go the same way others go, the man want to They try to maltreat them believing that if they do so; the women would not have the courage to do stupid things that some Nigerian women living in USA are notorious for. Some men even resort to verbal or physical abuse on these women that knew next to nothing about what life in USA is all about.

When these women finally get exposed to life here, and have some financial muscle, they decide flex their financial muscle. They try to get their own pound of flesh since they can now afford to threaten their men. And they went ahead and deal with the man at his own level, and thanks to American laws that makes women more powerful than men in America when it comes to domestic problems, at the end of the day, the man loose, and back to where he was 20 years ago, broke, disgusted, homeless and lonely with bad credit, can never go back to Nigeria to get another wife, the African American women here no longer want him again, he`s now a joke, if he wants sex now , he has to pay first before the underwear go down, and if he force it, he is going to spend the rest of his life in jail, and one more thing, the woman also is by herself taking of her children by herself with government support, nobody to have sex with her since she is used to holy sex, but there aren't one available here, and no white guys want to marry African woman, they can only pay you to fuck you, and trust this African women, they don`t like uncircumcised Philistine, they preferred going to sleep in church praying to get the man back or hope God will kill him for leaving when they sent her away, and since God is good in anointing CAIN , he always allows bad man to grow older in suffering while praying women raised up their kind themselves.

10. Some Mothers when they come to America will start taunting her hardworking daughter about how foolish the daughter was for letting her husband control her finances. She started advising her to open her own bank accounts. She said that it was her son-in-law's duty to take care of her daughter and not the other way round. She saw the pay check brought home every month by her daughter and was marveled. She told her daughter that all she makes does not

belong to the husband but to her family as she has to build a house in her father's house. She told her to start sending money home secretly to her father's house to enable them build a mansion in her father's house. If the lady stupidly and irresponsibly heeded to the advice of the mom. When the husband found out, they started having problems, some married women listen to lots of advises about how to deal with their husbands with regard to money issues... Some women that are already divorced from their husband, almost always do not feel very happy seeing other people who are enjoying blissful marriages. They are always envious of seeing other people succeed when they failed, and they needed the company of more Sisters in the Spirits who already settled to get marry to Jesus of Nazareth rather than Nigerian men.

11. What you want in life is different from whom you want, the struggle of life or the pursuit of happiness is always a battle of searching for what we want inside whom we want to be within a relationship but most of the time, the struggles always hinges on the fact that we tends not to get what we want from whom we want to associate with in life. Though some people in life do not know what they want, because if you know what you want you will recognized it when you see it, if you know whom you want, you will recognize him or her when you found met him or her for the first time and if you know where you are going, you will know it when you get there, and some are confused because they thought that whom they want will possessed what they want, so when they found whom they want, they keep going on searching for him or her

because they thought whom they want will always possessed everything they want when they finally found him or her, and those who like to pray expects that God will give them all what they want together with whom they want , but life is not like that, because in most cases , you do not get all what you want from the person whom you want, therefore , life struggles is torn between pursuing what you want in life , while staying with whom you want because the man you want may not have the ability to provide you all what you want, and this always bring crisis , nagging and problems in relationship .

12. The characteristics of LOVE become confused, when partners in relationship failed to recognized that LOVE does not exist in vacuum. LOVE reside in every man and woman, just like WAR reside in man or woman, LOVE cannot be seen, it reside inward woman and man , so if I am a thief and I fell in love with you, that does not stop me to steal from you, so the fact that I am stealing from you does not mean that I am not in love with you, if I am a liar, and in love with you, loving you will not stop me from telling you lies, if you are lazy and you are in love with me, I can be working 16 hours a day taking care of all the bills, why you sleep all day watching television, it's just that I am loved by a Lazy person, that does not mean you don`t love me, if you are a violent person, you can beat me up 2 hours ago, and when it comes to shut the door, here you roll close near me on bed wanting to do what? You just

cursed me out a couple of minutes ago, and now what? , I love you! , yes, you are love by a violent person, that does not take his love to you away from his heart, love therefore is express within the parameter of the lover`s character, attitude and disposition, so this love things does nothing else rather than expose your character to the other person you are in love with, My attitude is that I never call people on phone, so if I am in love with you, you better not measure my love by phone calling to check on you , even if you are out of my sight for weeks, so the fact that I did not call you on phone does not mean that I am not in love with you, my attitude is simply that I don`t call people on phone, so if you need a man that talks all the time on phone, then you may end up with someone who talks all jargons on phone but   a lazy man who cannot take care of you like me, so love comes with the character of the lover, so when you accept a lover , you just have to accept the total package, both the strength and the weakness of the lover, you cannot hate a part and reject the other, if you want a rich man, then you must have to accept all what comes with being married a rich man. If I am stingy, If I am an Adulterer, would a love to a woman makes me to be different, NO, I can be rich and She may still be a broke person, I can have 4 cars why he goes about by bus, because I don't know how to give or share what I have with others, such attitude will reflect towards those that I am in love with.

13. Many people are depressed , stressed and unhappy today, running around , working hard, or living a miserable life full of anxiety because whom they want did not match up with what they want out of life, some of us remain single because we are still looking for whom we want to possessed all what we want , so we keeping going out with whom we did not want , and using one eye to continue to search for the person who get what we want, but what our mother failed to tell us is that there is a protocol in heaven, that if you want God to answer your prayer in this world, you need to identified yourself with who needs your help because as long as you go about searching for that man who gets all what you want, you will be by yourself for a very long time to come, and many people are in marriage, fully married, but their mind is not settled in the marriage, because deep inside them, they are with this one, but their mind is still married to that one who does not exist anywhere, but in their thought , they thought had it been they waited a little bit more, they would have got that one , who will never show up till now if they had not married to this one they are with right now , but when you look at your Senior Sister, Grandma , Grandpa, Uncle , what suggest to you from their own experience that you would have got something better than the one you got now?.If life is so easy to give you all what you want in one basket, your senior brothers and sisters would have had it better

14. Life is a give and take, everybody needs help one way or the other, no man understand your own problem unless you told it to him, Pretty and feminine or attractive dresses alone will not keep a man, and the cold truth is that all good men this days in our capitalist society are older for single ladies, so if you want a man

that got all what you want, then he is going to be an older man , old enough to be your father or uncle, or probably got few children before she met you, and if you want someone of your own age, then he probably ends up to be your student at home about things pertaining to life, so you have to be ready to marry to a boy until he grow to become a man and if you nag him too much, trying to force him to grow up to become a man, he may end up leaving you and you end up by yourself taking care of your babies alone. You are not going to get all what you want in whom you want; you have to make a choice, whether it is whom you want that is most important to you or what you want.

The old Prophet and the Young Prophet.

The current problem in Nigeria today is more or less like the bible story recorded in 1 Kings Chapter 13 of the Bible, a story of a young Prophet called a man of God from Judah and one Old Prophet. This young junior Prophet gave a prophetic statement to the nation and because it was not pleasing to the King, The king stretched his hand that he should be arrested, and the hand stretched towards the man of God was paralyzed, the King then beg for prayer from same man of God, the man prayed for the King and the King hand was restored, the King then invited the man of God to Dinner, and for a gift, But in verse 8 **of the book** the man of God answered the king, "Even if you were to give me half your possessions, I would not go with you, nor would I eat bread or drink water here. [9] For I was commanded by the word of the LORD: 'You must not eat bread or drink water or return by the way you came.'" [10] So he took another road and did not return by the way he had come to Bethel.

Verse 11: Now there was a certain old prophet living in Bethel, whose sons came and told him all that the man of God had done there that day. They also told their father what he had said to the king.

[12] Their father asked them, "Which way did he go?" And his sons showed him which road the man of God from Judah had taken. The Old Prophet, that is the experienced most Senior Prophet, Evangelist and Apostle ran after this Junior Prophet who though

48

called by God and anointed by God and fear no one and did obey what God told him to do or say to the nation , but he was ignorant about the politics of religion and the governance of the state fell into the trap of trying to listen to the advice of the elder prophet, so the Older Prophet came after the this young prophet "Are you the man of God who came from Judah?" "I am," he replied.

[15] So the old prophet / most senior evangelist said to this new man of God in town, "Come home with me and eat." [16] The man of God said, "I cannot turn back and go with you, nor can I eat bread or drink water with you in this place. [17] I have been told by the word of the LORD: 'You must not eat bread or drink water there or return by the way you came.'". I said this to the Politician at the state house, now I am saying the same thing to you in the Church, I am only going to do what God told me to do, then 18 The old prophet answered, "I too am a prophet, founder of this church from heaven, anointed and most senior in this nation, when I give instruction to you, forget about what God told you

You have just started hearing from God, I have been hearing the voice of God and seeing Angels visiting me from heaven before you were born, Listen to me young man of God, An angel said to me by the word of the LORD: 'Bring him back with you to your house so that he may eat bread and drink water.'" (But he was lying to him.) [19] So this young man of God returned with the old man of God and ate and drank in the Elder prophet house. (Because as a Junior Prophet, he did not know that God calling is generational, that he call people for different generations, he call your fathers for their own generation, he has call you for your own generation, the calling of God has no repentance, so your father in the Lord cannot tell you that you must worship, serve or do the church thing the way God and Angels told me him to do it, you have to perfect your own ministries the way God told you to do it for your own generations).

Verse 20: While they were sitting at the table, the word of the LORD came to the old prophet who had brought him back. [21] He cried out to the man of God who had come from Judah, "This is what the LORD says: 'You have defied the word of the LORD and have not kept the command the LORD your God gave you. (Mind you, it was this old man that pressurize and convinced and encouraged this young man of God to do it his own way against the way God told this young man.)

[22] You came back and ate bread and drank water in the place where God told you not to eat or drink because an elderly man of God told you to do what is against your own purpose, destiny and assignment for your own generation? Therefore your body will not be buried in the tomb of your ancestors.'"

Verse 23: When the man of God had finished eating and drinking, the prophet who had brought him back saddled his donkey for him. [24] As he went on his way, a lion met him on the road and killed him, and his body was left lying on the road, with both the donkey and the lion standing beside it.

[25] Some people who passed by saw the body lying there, with the lion standing beside the body, and they went and reported it in the city where the old prophet lived. He died a PUBLIC DISGRACEFUL DEATH WITHOUT FULFILLING HIS MINISTRY AND PURPOSE ON EARTH, why? He did not do what God told him to do, but occupied himself following the order of the Most Superior Senior Prophet, that is why Paul told the believers , if Angels come from heaven and told you something else beside these thing, do not believe them, because it is dangerous for you to hear the voice of God, and put it aside and

you get busy with a system of worship and religious order handed down by your father, all because you want to obey the way it was set down from heaven to your father in the Lord .Verse 26: When the Most Senior Evangelist/ Primate/ Founder prophet who had brought him back from his journey heard of it, he said, "It is the man of God who defied the word of the LORD. The LORD has given him over to the lion, which has mauled him and killed him, as the word of the LORD had warned him." BUT HE DISOBEYED GOD because he was trying to follow your order of church service handed over to you by the Angeles from heaven.

[30] Then he laid the body in his own tomb, and they mourned over him in the wake-keeping and funeral service and said, "Alas, my brother!"

That old prophet deceived the other ministers, who came to become members and ministers in the Church he founded. The man of God who was *deceived* thought he was OBEYING GOD by obeying the old Prophet, but he wasn't! Let me emphasize that again, the man who was deceived thought he was OBEYING GOD, but he , he was actually being led into sin! Because He did not understand that God calling is generational, God has call you for your own generation, do not let the respect of your father and mother or respect to elders or respect to men of God stop you from what God is telling you to do for this time. This is your time; this is your moment, ACT NOW! The young prophet was completely SINCERE and wanted God's will, but was misled by a message supposedly from God from another man of God who is senior in rank to him and older and more experienced than him, and more recognized and popular than him. I am call by God to serve the people, I will not take instructions from any traditional rulers or religious leaders to do what God has sent me to do to make the necessary changes that this nation deserved, Searching for the truth is the most honorable ministry in this world, and it`s my most dangerous assignment. God that has begin a good work through me will complete in his appointed time leaving a legacy that will endure into eternity.

JUDAISM, CHRISTIANITY & ISLAM and How to become a Citizen of Heaven

Judaism is a religion whose core believes and commission is to protects the survival of the Jewish people, The Jews having experienced the slavery in Egypt , followed by 40 years desert struggle to years of waiting for the Messiah to deliver the Jews from the persecution of surrounding enemies and the Romans government, the core believes of the Jewish people has been that of survival, the religion of Judaism becomes a commission after the holocaust, a commission that every Jews must fight to survive from extermination in this Planet , fight socially, politically and economically , even if it required you as a Jew to marry your own Sister as a Wife or as an Husband, so Judaism today has nothing to do with preaching to take anybody to heaven, anything spiritual about the Judaism in our world today is point towards worldly success politically , economically , militarily and estate planning for your own children or to the next generation of the Jewish people, that is why today some Jews do not care if Judaism is mixed up with being a member of a Lodge, Rosicrucian or a member of the Scottish Rite organization etc. or even being a member of a Secret society provided it can guaranteed your success financially, politically or to maintain a high influential position or able to influence political, judicial or legislative decisions in our world today in a way that no religion or government on earth will ever rise up to the level of repeating the holocaust again in our world.

ISLAM

Islam is a religion of Protection of Morality, Culture, tradition , Land , Possession and the Man Ancient laws, rules and regulation , its commission is to protect its followers from the religion of grace that Christianity is all about and also to protect itself from the unapologetic commission of Judaism whose commission is to stop any power from ever rising up again to try the experience of holocaust, Islam is afraid of Christianity message of grace that will give freedom to women and the teenagers and the young adults in their society thereby make useless the ancient rules of morality that says whatever you do , you must suffer for it and died for it, though it has its root believe in same God of Christianity , it s problem is not about Jesus Christ, its problem is the fact that there is no grace or forgiveness for sinners, you must suffer for it in this world and in the afterlife, you will be rejected by God as sinners, so what Islam is fighting against in Christianity is the message of Grace And some Pastors behave like Osama Bin Laden when they preach to oppose the message of grace in their denomination.

The notion of God's love coming to us free of charge, no strings attached, seems to go against every instinct of humanity. The Buddhist eight-fold path, the Hindu doctrine of Karma, the Jewish covenant, and the Muslim code of law—each of these offers a way to earn approval. Only Christianity dares to make God's love

54

unconditional, I can NEVER DO ENOUGH to deserve salvation. Muslim believes that One day we're all going to die, and God's going to judge us, [our] good and bad deeds. [If the] bad outweighs the good, you go to hell; if the good outweighs the bad, you go to heaven." That's what many people believe. But that's not what the Bible says.

The bible says:

"For by grace you have been saved through faith—and this not from yourselves. It is the gift of God—not by works, so that no one can boast" (Eph. 2:8-9).

CHRISTIANITY

Christianity is a religion of Grace , it embraces poverty, it respects and gives place and hope to the common people through its core believes that centered on a place calls heaven - a life after life, a believes system that says that you don`t have to bother or worry about your financial, economic or political status or suffering or fighting for survival in this world, just believes in God of heaven through his Son a Jew who came to this world about 2000 years ago, he already died for your sin, whatever may be your sin, your disease or struggle , all what you have to do is just accept the fact that he died for your sin, so by mere believe and faith in the fact that his suffering , death , resurrection and accession has completed your own process of a ticket to heaven where he is now, guaranteed you a place with God after this life , therefore your life in this world is temporary compare with eternity with

God in Heaven, and you don't get this opportunity to be adopted as a child of God because of the good work you have done in this flesh, but it's by grace, and the Christianity commissions is go to all the world and preach this same message of grace to everyone, even with empty stomach, even while you are suffering to pay the church mortgage and bills.

In the Bible we find God's moral law. The only way for me to be saved on my own would be to perfectly obey every one of God's commands. But that's impossible. I'm far from perfect. "Whoever keeps the whole law and yet stumbles at just one point is guilty of breaking all of it" (James 2:10).

"We know that whatever the law says, it says to those who are under the law, so that every mouth may be silenced and the whole world held accountable to God. Therefore no one will be declared righteous in his sight by observing the law; rather, through the law we become conscious of sin" (Rom. 3:19).

So, I need to be saved by grace. I need undeserved salvation. Christ DID ENOUGH to provide salvation for me. God deals favorably with people in a way they do not deserve. The only other principle by which God can deal with people is law. This principle requires Him to deal with people in a way they deserve. Since sinners deserve hell, they cannot be delivered from this penalty by law. The spiritual blindness of man is evident in that all their religions teach that people are saved by their works, the very principle which bars them from acceptance with God. No one can ever be saved from his sins apart from God's grace.

What has Jesus done for me?

A. SUBSTITUTION: Jesus died in my place. "Christ died for sins once for all, the righteous for the unrighteous, to bring you to God. He was put to death in the body but made alive by the Spirit" (1 Peter 3:18).

B. JUSTIFICATION: Jesus made me right with God. "He was delivered over to death for our sins and was raised to life for our justification" (Rom. 4:25). Justification: God sees me just as if I had never sinned. I'm innocent, no longer guilty.

C. RECONCILIATION: Jesus made peace with God possible. "God was reconciling the world to himself in Christ, not counting men's sins against them" (2 Cor. 5:19). Jesus is the bridge between God and man.

D. ADOPTION: Jesus made me a part of God's family. *"He predestined us to be adopted as his sons through Jesus Christ, in accordance with his pleasure and will"* (Eph. 1:5).

E. REDEMPTION: Jesus purchased my salvation with his blood.

The Greek word for redemption refers to slaves being purchased in the marketplace. In the spiritual sense, all of us were slaves to sin until Jesus purchased us out of the slave market and set us free from sin's bondage. Because He bought us and paid for us with His blood, we now belong exclusively to Him.

"For you know that it was not with perishable things such as silver or gold that you were redeemed from the empty way of life handed down to you from your forefathers, but with the precious blood of Christ, a lamb without blemish or defect" (1 Peter 1:18-19).

F. PROPITIATION: Jesus satisfied God's justice. To propitiate is to bring satisfaction or to fulfill a demand or requirement. In heathen circles it was a word that meant "to appease the gods." The biblical sense of the word speaks of that which satisfies the justice of God so that mercy is given. "He is the atoning sacrifice [propitiation] for our sins and not only for ours but also for the sins of the whole world" (1 John 2:2). "This is love: not that we loved God, but that he loved us and sent his Son as an atoning sacrifice for our sins" (1 John 4:10).

G. FORGIVENESS: Jesus sent my sins away from me. "In him we have redemption through his blood, the forgiveness of sins, in accordance with the riches of God's grace" (Eph. 1:7). "All have sinned and fall short of the glory of God, and are justified freely by his grace through the redemption that came by Christ Jesus" (Rom. 3:23-24).

And so, when you look at the cross and see Jesus hanging there, what you don't hear is "Earn this." What He says is "I chose this. You don't have to pay anything for it"

Grace is often defined by using the five letters of the word: God's Riches at Christ's Expense.

III. Salvation is a GIFT for me to RECEIVE, not a REWARD for me to EARN.

"The wages of sin is death, but the gift of God is eternal life in Christ Jesus our Lord" (Rom. 6:23).

How do I receive the gift of salvation?

• By ADMITTING that I am a sinner.

• By BELIEVING that Jesus Christ died for my sins and rose from the grave.

• By CALLING to God for salvation.

These are the ABC's of salvation: Admit, Believe, and Call.

If you would like to receive God's gift of salvation today, would you please repeat this prayer after me:

Jesus, I admit to you that I am a sinner.
I believe that you died on the cross for my sin
and rose again to save me.
Today I give my life to you.

Please save me.
Thank You.
Amen.

"For by grace you have been saved through faith—and this not from yourselves—it is the gift of God—not by works, so that no one can boast" (Eph. 2:8).

After you are adopted as a Citizen of heaven, your are then given a measure of faith and the indwelling holy spirit to begin your relationship with your father as a newly adopted member of the family, the way and manner you use your faith and cooperate with the holy spirit is what is going to determine the level of your activities in this world and your reward.

WHY AFRICAN CHURCHES SUFFERED GROWTH IN AMERICA

"A large appetite is gluttony in the Greeks, but in the Gauls it is nature." Again, the Egyptians and the Syrians, in their hot climate, did not need active employment in the same way as the western nations do, in order to keep their minds and their bodies healthful. They could spend their hours and their days in calmly thinking of spiritual things, or of nothing at all, in a way which the more active mind of Europeans and the Americans cannot bear. And again, many rules as to dress, which are suitable for one sort of climate, are quite unfit for a different sort. Christianity had made its way into most other countries of the world. We may stop to take a view of some things connected with the Church; and it will be well, in doing so, to remember what is wisely said the practices handed down in the Church is not necessary that traditions and ceremonies be the same as one in all the places of the world, and utterly alike; for at all times they have been divers" (that is, they have differed in different parts of Christ's Church), "and they may be changed according to the diversities of countries, times, and men's manners, so that nothing be ordained against God's Word.". Church worship cannot be the same way given considerations to different culture and traditions in different countries of the world, but one thing must be the same FROM THE AGE OF THE APOSTLES is that every Christian must be filled with the HOLY SPIRIT , which is the beginning of the Christian Church as reckoned from the great day on which the Holy Ghost came down, upon devout men out of every nation under heaven," when gathered together at Jerusalem, at the upper room , they returned to their own countries, they carried back with them the news of the wonderful things which had taken place at Jerusalem. After this, the Apostles went forth "into the entire world, "as their Master had ordered them, to "preach the Gospel to every creature". The Church begins with the Holy Ghost upon men who gathered in the church that day; follow by Paul preaching in Asia Minor, Greece, and at Rome, while the other Apostles were busily doing the same work in other countries. However we must consider how merchants travelled from country to country on account of their trade; how soldiers were sent into all quarters of the empire and were moved about from one country to another. And from these things we may get some understanding of how Christianity has been mixed up with wars and the pursuit of materials things of this world, but the real thing is that you must be born again and be filled with Holy Ghost power from above.

The Church has come alive to this stage, because in every generations one after the other, a man of God arises and make a little change to depart from what the older generations laid down as church doctrine and system of worship, but it is rather unfortunate that this generations has since stick to old methods of doing things in our generations. The way you do church in Nigeria or Ghana or way back in your Country cannot work here in America because the practices handed down in the Church are not necessary that traditions and ceremonies be the same as one in all the places of the world.

Nigerians cannot govern themselves under the current leadership, Terrorism always gains sanctuary in ungoverned spaces and start to build a terrorist infrastructure, and then the threat of the terrorist launching attacks grows. With Boko Haram kidnapping of some 270 school girls and threats to sell them into sexual slavery is a clear indication that the battles of Nigeria has shifted from a fight between the good luck people and the bad luck people and it has now becomes a battle of the gods, a truth which has now sparked international outrage, leading to pledges of assistance to Nigeria. France has once again offered its help, China is willing to share satellite imagery that might help locate the militants, and Britain has offered its Special Air Service commandos and surveillance aircraft. USA is sending a multiagency counterterrorism team that includes FBI hostage negotiators and investigators, intelligence analysts, and up to 10 uniformed personnel from the U.S. Africa Command to assess the military needs of the Nigerian security forces. The mass kidnapping of children, combined with other recent attacks — including a bombing in a bus station in Nigeria's capital of Abuja that killed more than 70 people and a massacre at an open-air market in the northern city of Gamboru Ngala that reportedly killed more than 300 civilians has crossed a new threshold of lethality and depravity that there is a political power vacuum in this ungoverned nation of Nigeria , the power that govern Nigeria is hidden behind religion and traditional rulers institutions , not the political power led by the President of the Country. A Nigerian soldier or Police man or a member of Nigerian Security forces who died as a result of trying to save another Nigerian will be a laughing stock to the rest Nigerians because Nigeria is a country that has no place for Heroes , the only person Nigerians respect and honor is a person with money, big mansions , expensive cars and high costs clothes and attires, Nigerian culture put the Nigerian military and the security forces in a corner not to want to die in an efforts to save another Nigerians.